CW00545657

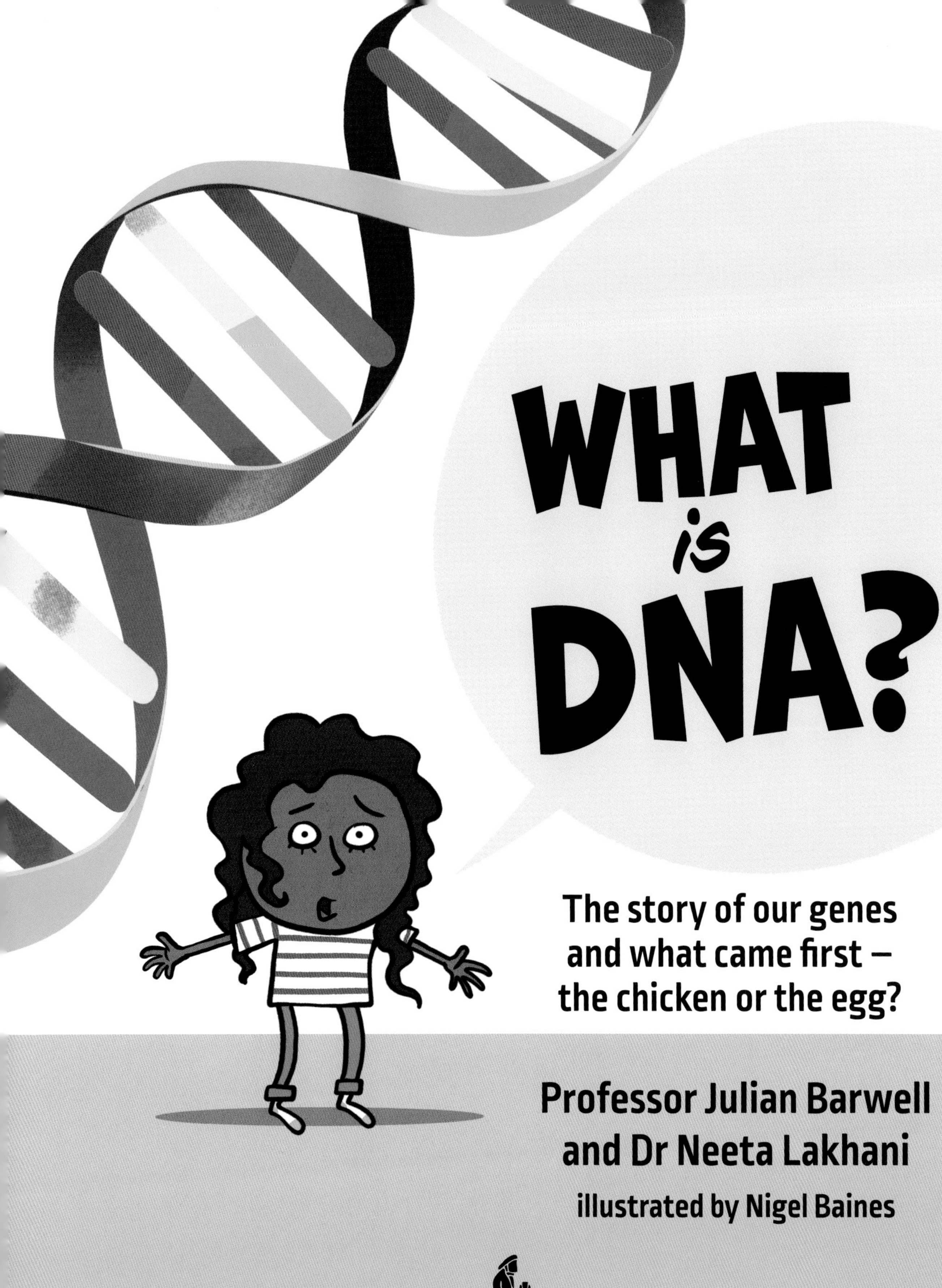

WHAT *is* DNA?

The story of our genes and what came first – the chicken or the egg?

Professor Julian Barwell and Dr Neeta Lakhani

illustrated by Nigel Baines

WAYLAND

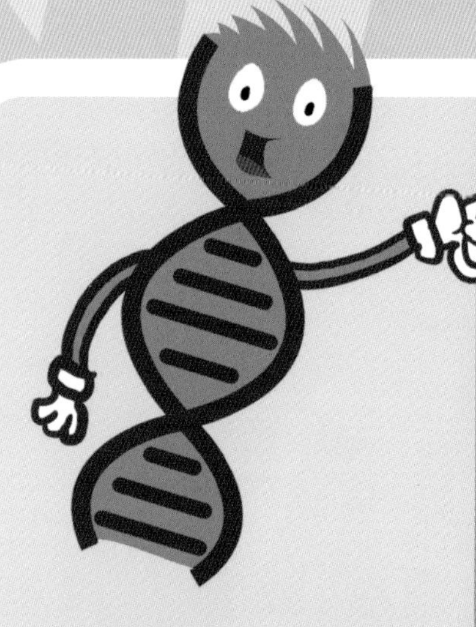

INTRODUCTION

The study of genes and DNA is a voyage of discovery that will take you from the beginnings of life on Earth billions of years ago through to explaining why some of us really don't like vegetables – and why some of us love them!

The book describes how a chemical called DNA is the building block of all kinds of life. That includes all animals like us humans, but also trees and seaweed – even the vegetables you ate for lunch! DNA has been passed from parents to their offspring – or children – from generation to generation over millions of years.

- You will learn about the structure of the DNA chemical and see how it works inside your body.
- How did life begin on Earth? You'll find out that all living things are connected by their DNA – some more than others.
- Next we'll discuss how DNA carries a coded set of instructions for building a human body. We all have a unique set of instructions given to us by our parents. This is called inheritance, and it has a very big impact on what you look like.
- Finally, the book shows how understanding the role of DNA in the world around us can be used to do many things, such as create better medicines and vaccines – and even solve crimes!

Dedicated to Despina, Marina, Nicholas and Anna

First published in Great Britain in 2024 by Wayland

Editor: Tom Jackson
Design and illustration: Nigel Baines

The authors would like to thank Vanessa, Kiran, Eleanor, Julie, Ron, Shirley, Simon, Peter and the pupils at Catmose College, Rutland, UK.

ISBN (HB): 978 1 5263 2299 9
ISBN (PB): 978 1 5263 2300 2
ISBN (ebook): 978 1 5263 2632 4

Printed and bound in China

Wayland, an imprint of
Hachette Children's Group
Part of Hodder and Stoughton
Carmelite House
50 Victoria Embankment
London EC4Y 0DZ
An Hachette UK Company

www.hachette.co.uk
www.hachettechildrens.co.uk

CONTENTS

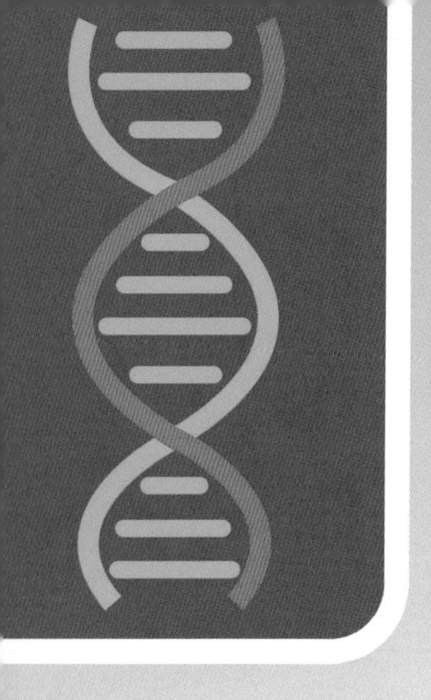

WELCOME TO THE LANGUAGE

There are only four letters!

A...G...C...T
Oi! What do you think you're doing?
Sugars! Yum!

DNA is a special code that carries the **instruction manual to build a human**. It uses an alphabet with only four letters, and these are stuck together with a special sugar paste to make the recipe for the human body. DNA is a very long **chemical**, shaped like a **twisting ladder**, that is made up of the **four letters** strung together. There are copies of this chemical inside every cell in our body.

OF LIFE

Welcome to the great discovery of DNA. DNA is the code, or language, inside us that we have inherited from our parents and may pass on if we have children. It shapes who we are!

What is this DNA thing? Is it a spring?
This body isn't right at all. I'll need to use the DNA instructions and start again.

We are given our **DNA letters** from our parents to help build our bodies. Tiny changes in the order of these letters make us all different from each other and other living organisms.

The DNA recipe to make a human connects us to each other and all living things right the way back to the beginning of life on Earth.

In this book, you will find out how DNA explains how tall you are, the **colour of your hair**, whether you like certain **vegetables** and even how you behave at times.

You'll also discover whether grandad really is a dinosaur and, of course, what came first – the **chicken or the egg**. But first, let's find out how we know about DNA ...

THE GREAT

How do we know about DNA and how to read it?

James Watson and **Francis Crick** were the scientists that first announced to the world in 1953 that they had cracked the secret of the structure of DNA.

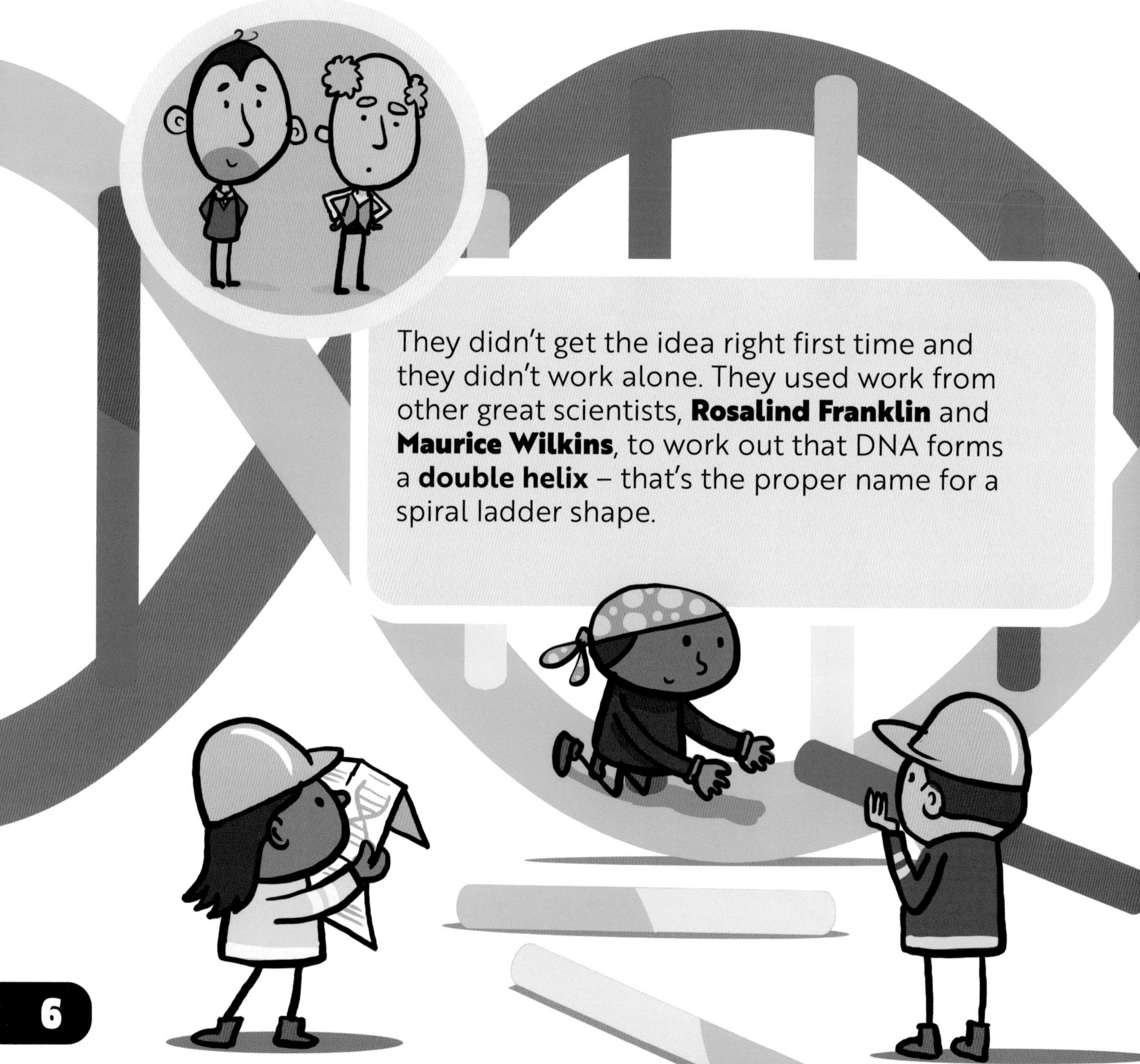

They didn't get the idea right first time and they didn't work alone. They used work from other great scientists, **Rosalind Franklin** and **Maurice Wilkins**, to work out that DNA forms a **double helix** – that's the proper name for a spiral ladder shape.

DISCOVERY!

Pairing up

The helix is made of two chains of DNA's letters **A, T, C,** and **G**. These two strands are strung into a ladder-shape by pairs of the letters linked together. Crick and Watson found that the letters always work in the same pairs. **A** links with **T** and **C** links with **G**.

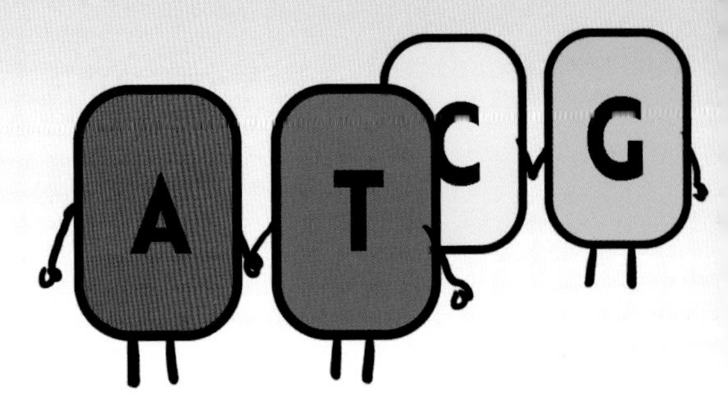

Making copies

The ladder-like system means that the body can **copy DNA** very easily. The second strand is made by pairing up letters with the first strand. It is a bit like taking a picture of **a reflection in a mirror** that can be used for copying.

THE CODE
THE MACHINES

How are our instructions used?

DNA provides the recipe to build the body. The body is built from small units called cells, and each cell has its own copy of DNA stored in a library called the **nucleus**.

My DNA is safe in here.

The code is divided into separate instructions called **genes**. Each gene is a sequence of letters like the words in a sentence. The genes are stored on chromosomes, which are a bit like a full story.

We have two sets of genes, one from Mum and one from Dad. The genes are read by code breakers called **ribosomes** to make complicated chemicals called **proteins**. Proteins are the **chemical machines** that do all the jobs inside the cells and all over the body.

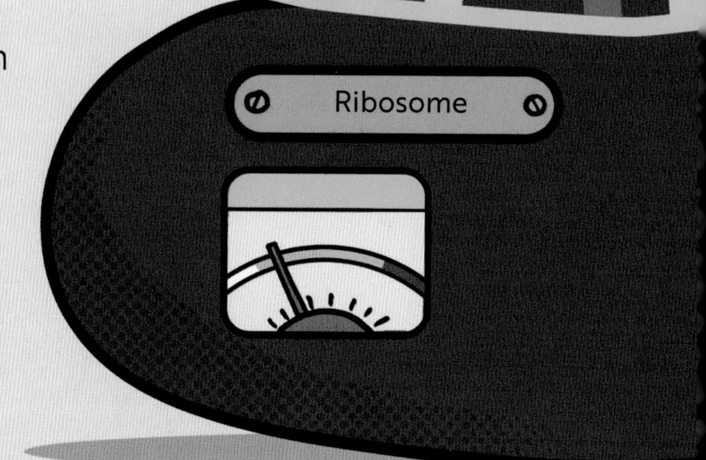
Ribosome

BREAKERS AND INSIDE OUR BODIES

Breaking the code

The two strands in the double helix break apart and a gene is copied from the DNA code. That copy heads out of the nucleus to the ribosomes waiting in a cell's protein factory, which is called the **endoplasmic reticulum**, or ER for short.

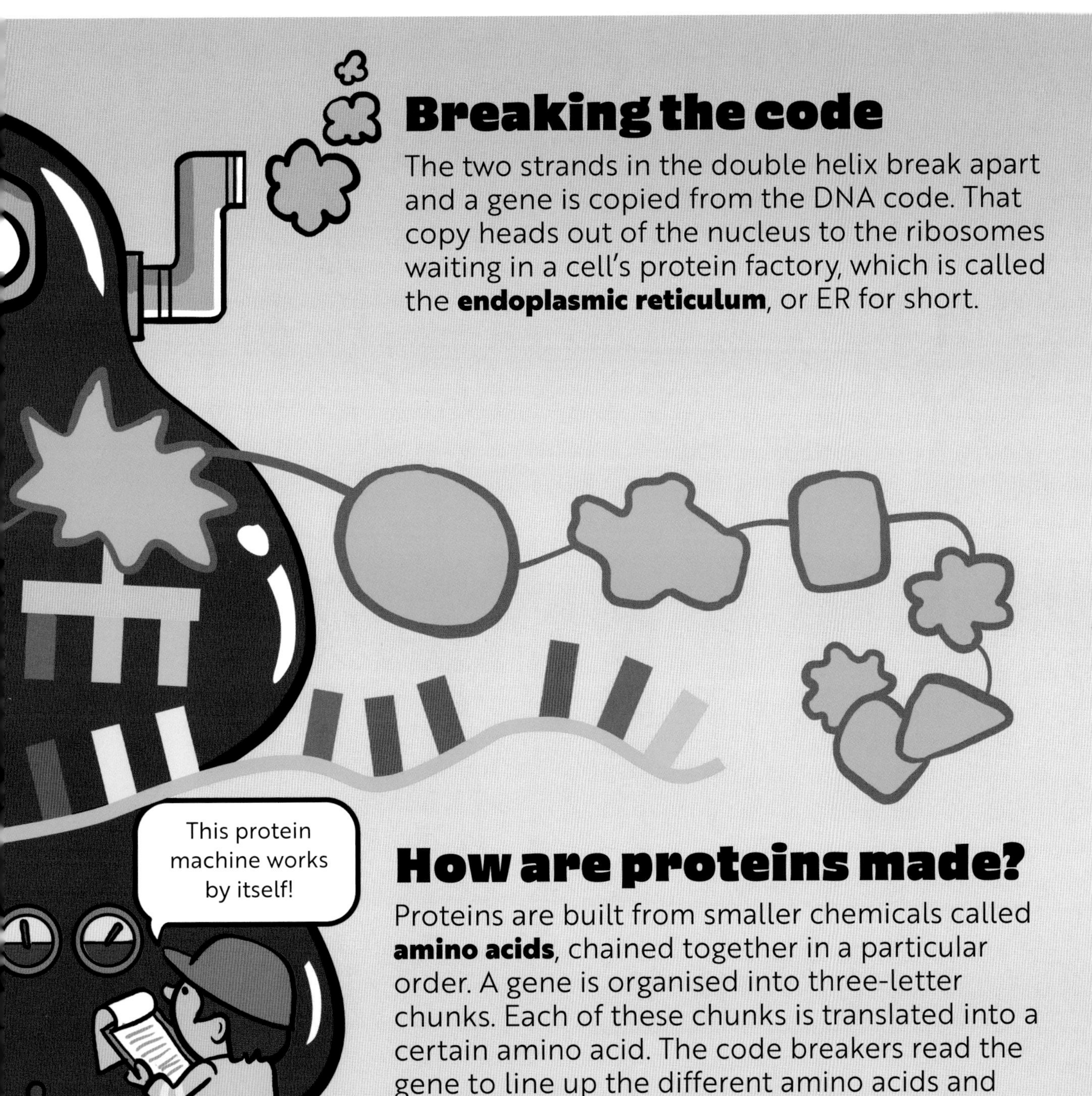
This protein machine works by itself!

How are proteins made?

Proteins are built from smaller chemicals called **amino acids**, chained together in a particular order. A gene is organised into three-letter chunks. Each of these chunks is translated into a certain amino acid. The code breakers read the gene to line up the different amino acids and connect them together to make the protein.

BABIES COME WITH INSTRUCTIONS

So, how come some babies are boys and others are girls?

You are so small! Do you do anything?
Of course!
X chromosome
Y chromosome

Our DNA is stored in **46 really long strands called chromosomes**. The chromosomes come in pairs, with one set coming from each of our parents.

That means we end up with a library of genes containing two copies of the same 23 chromosomes. One of the pairs is special. Mum always gives us a chromosome called X, and Dad supplies either an **X or a Y chromosome**, so our library either has two Xs or X and Y. If Dad passes on a Y chromosome, the baby will be born a boy. If the baby has two X chromosomes it will be a girl.

GENE LIBRARY
So, you've got NOTHING here on football?

Sperm
Egg
I told you we shouldn't have stopped for a rest!

Dividing time

A boy or girl is made when the **sperm from Dad** joins with the **egg from Mum**. When the egg and sperm join together they produce a single cell which then divides into two cells, then four, then eight, then 16 cells, and soon creates a very early stage of a baby called an **embryo**. The cells will divide again about **40 times over nine months** to create a baby human.

Excellent. Now, if you could just do it again 40 times.

IS IT GOOD TO

How we pass on our genes as our cells divide

As the body grows, our cells divide so one cell turns into two new ones. This process is called **mitosis**. All chromosomes are copied perfectly before the cells split in two, so each new cell has the **normal double set of 46 chromosomes**. Mitosis is happening right now inside you as your body makes new cells.

STAGE 0

Cells are splitting inside me?!

STAGE 1

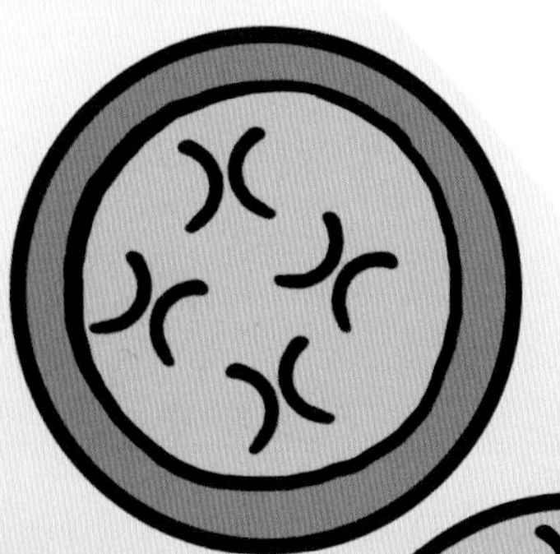

In dividing cells, chromosomes first copy and double the amount of DNA and this folds up really tight and become more visible

STAGE 2

Chromosomes line up in the centre

STAGE 3

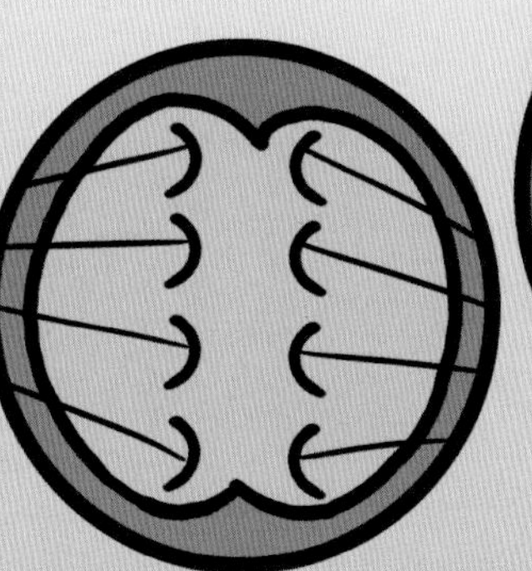

Chromosomes pulled apart

STAGE 4

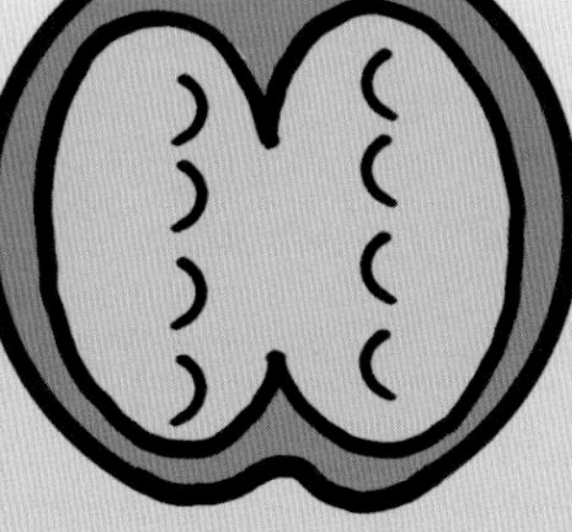

Cell divides

STAGE 5

Separate chromosomes

Two new cells (identical to stage 0)!

MIX UP OUR DNA?

How do we make new life?

To make babies, our cells divide by a different process called **meiosis**. It is used to make the sperm and eggs that go on to create babies. The starting cell splits into **four new cells**. Each of these new cells ends up with just a single set of **23 chromosomes**, half as many as the starting cell. When a baby is made, a sperm and egg join together, and their 23 chromosomes are added together to make a full set of 46.

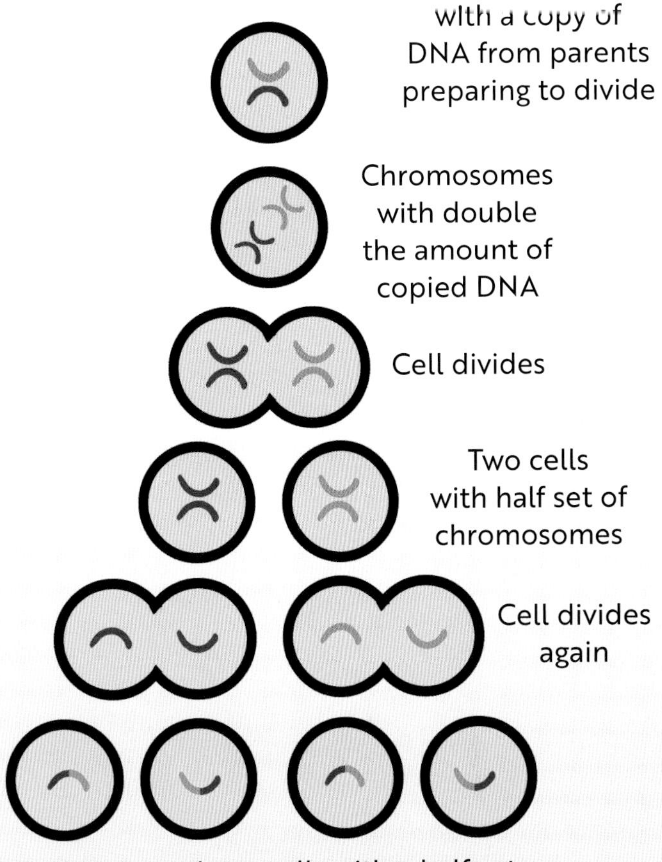

This system of divisions is there to make sure that each of us gets a **unique set of genes**, half from Mum and the other half from Dad.

Mixing genes into new sets is a good idea because it gives us a chance of **inheriting useful genes** from one parent that will take over from any unhelpful genes from the other. A varied set of genes helps us stay alive and keep healthy!

HOW ARE TWINS MADE?

Copy kids

Identical twins are amazing because they are two people with the **same DNA**. Scientists like to study twins because it helps us to understand what genes do.

Identical twins are formed when one egg from Mum and one sperm from Dad join together and then splits completely in two to make two embryos. The twins have exactly the same DNA, they look very similar and can be hard to tell apart.

Some twins are non-identical. **Non-identical twins** occur when two eggs are released from Mum and are met by two different sperm. Because of this, non-identical twins do not have exactly the same DNA as each other.

Twin tests

Speaking to different sets of identical twins is a useful way to understand how much our genes control what we look like, what we do and how healthy we are. Twins generally grow up together and so they may be similar not because of their identical genes, but because they both live in the same place. Doctors and scientists love to **study twins** that grew up in different homes so they can really see the effect that genes have.

HOW DID LIFE

A soup of chemicals

A lot of different scientists and religions have ideas about how life began. **No one really knows.** However, scientists have been carrying out experiments and think it is possible that life may have started by a process nicknamed the **'soup theory'**.

The idea is that Earth started out with a mixture of **simple chemical ingredients** mixed into water. This was heated up by the Sun, and lightning added sparks of electricity. Very gradually the ingredients began to join together making more complicated substances. Eventually they made DNA! DNA has the amazing **ability to copy itself**, using raw ingredients in the chemical soup around it. Maybe this is how life begins?

Yeuch! It was horrible in there!

ON EARTH BEGIN?

It is a bit like mixing eggs, flour, butter and sugar and then adding heat to make a cake – which is very different to its raw ingredients. Scientists have tried to **recreate the beginning of life** on Earth by mixing the raw ingredients they think might have been around before life began. They have found that the simplest chemicals needed by living organisms do form in the mixture, but so far nothing as complicated as DNA has appeared.

Well, we haven't *quite* created life as yet, but we came pretty close with this chocolate cake

WHAT CAME FIRST – THE CHICKEN

Looking for the relations

In 1859 British naturalist **Charles Darwin** came up with an idea called **natural selection**.

I've had an idea!

If it involves going sailing again, forget it.

He sailed around the world observing how living things that are strong, fast or have other features that help them to **survive** are more likely to have their own offspring. Their successful skills and features are passed on to their offspring.

Darwin called this 'natural selection' and he explained how it meant life **evolved**, or changed slowly, over millions of years by being flexible enough to **adapt to the world** around it.

Natural selection in action

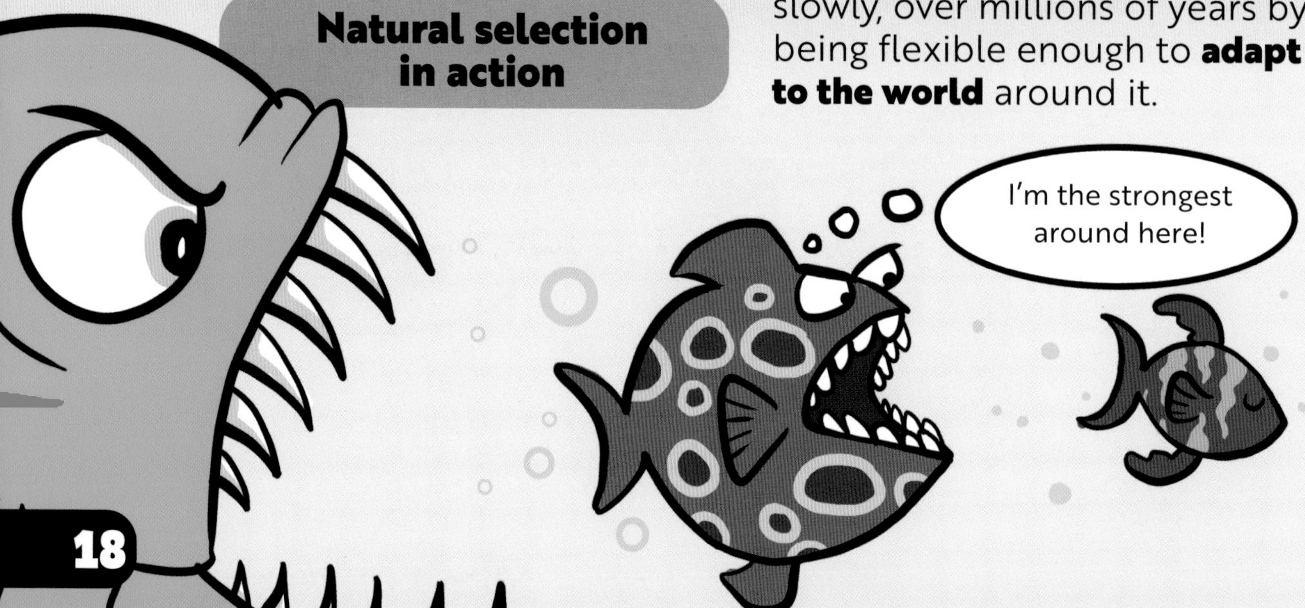

I'm the strongest around here!

OR THE EGG?

We now know that a parent's genes are passed onto offspring through DNA. By comparing the **genetic code** of similar animals, we can read the history book of life! For instance, scientists have discovered that **chickens** are more closely related to **dinosaurs** than they are to crocodiles or humans. That means birds and dinosaurs evolved from the same **ancestor**.

A dinosaur-like creature laid an egg with some small changes to its DNA that made it look more like a chicken. Over millions of years many more small changes added up to create the first chicken – **so the egg came first**!

I thought eggs usually got beaten, NOT chickens!

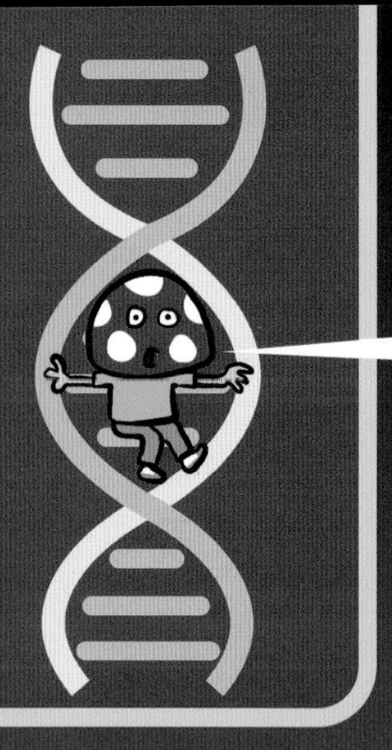

ARE WE 50% A

Using DNA to look back in time

Sorry I'm late. The interstellar traffic was a nightmare.

Astronomers can look at stars billions of kilometres away to study the beginning of time as the light released from them in the past is reaching us now.

To study humans from the distant past **historians** read old books and visit old buildings, while **archaeologists** dig up ancient tools, coins or pottery.

Fossils are the remains of dead life that have turned to stone. Scientists can **measure their age** from the way chemicals inside have changed. It is a bit like the way you can tell how old food is by how mouldy it is!

MUSHROOM?

We can use DNA to show how life has evolved over millions of years. DNA develops random changes, called **mutations**, that appear at the same speed over many millions of years. The number of different mutations in the DNA codes of two life forms shows us how long ago the two evolved from the **same ancestor**. All life is related in some way. The system tells us that humans share 80% of their DNA with dogs and even 50% with mushrooms. So you could say we are half mushroom!

We also know that our **oldest gene** is two billion years old. All of today's animals, plants and mushrooms evolved from an ancestor that lived way back then. We are older than we might think!

80% dog

60% banana

50% mushroom

IS GRANDAD

Where do we come from?

One hundred years ago your eight great-grandparents (three **generations** back) would probably have been alive. If you go back further, over 600 years and 25 generations, this means over **four million of your relatives** that directly made you were alive somewhere on Earth.

1422
Wow! I might get 600 years' worth of birthday presents!
TIME MACHINE
WOOOOSH

REALLY A DINOSAUR?

Our relations

Modern **humans evolved** from animals about 200,000 years ago (about 10,000 generations). By comparing the codes in DNA and looking at how many people were likely to be around 200,000 years ago, we can see that all humans alive today are closely related to each other and to similar mammals like **chimpanzees** and **gorillas**.

Dinosaurs were **reptiles** that became **extinct** 66 million years ago. Grandad was not made by a dinosaur, but both do share a common ancestor if you go back far enough. And because we are constantly evolving very slowly, Grandad's DNA is a bit more like a dinosaur's than yours!

Grandad, what ... er ... big horns you have!

WHY DON'T I

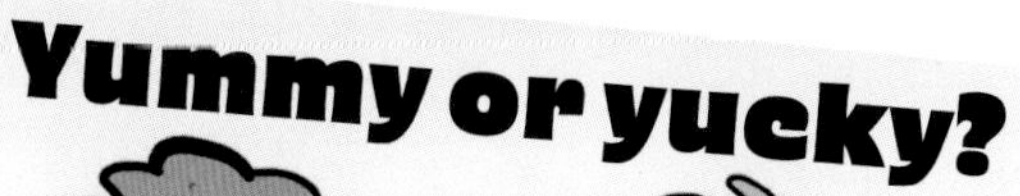

Yummy or yucky?

We're not keen on you either!

How come some people love to eat bitter **green vegetables** like Brussels sprouts while some people cannot stand the taste of them?

Why do some people have **blue eyes** while others have **brown eyes?**

Why do some people have **ginger hair** while others have **black hair?**

You've had my comb for an hour!

We think all of these answers may have something to do with

GENES ...

LIKE VEGETABLES?

We all have about 20,000 genes that are inherited from our parents or are newly made (called de novo) when we are created.

These genes can help determine things such as hair colour and risk of medical conditions.

WHY CAN I/CAN'T I ROLL MY TONGUE?

Sometimes inheriting a single copy of a gene, such as the gene for being able to roll your tongue (R), is enough to change the make-up of our body. This is called an **autosomal dominant effect.** Autosomal means it doesn't matter which parent gives you the gene.

If Mum has one copy of the R gene and one copy of the non-roll N gene, and Dad has two copies of N, there is a chance you will inherit the R gene from your mother, making you roll your tongue (although you can improve with practice and, in reality, a number of genes are involved).

But, not all genes work like this ...

HOW DID I GET

Why are we so different?

Other types of characteristics, such as ginger hair (or blue eyes), only occur when we **inherit** a change in a gene from both parents. This is called an **autosomal recessive effect.** Having just one copy of a brown-hair gene (B) is enough to have brown hair, but people with ginger hair inherit the same red-hair gene (R) from BOTH Mum and Dad.

Red-haired people have two copies of the red-hair gene.

BUT WHAT ABOUT VEGETABLES?

Two copies of a **supertaster gene** make Brussels sprouts taste bitter. One copy is not enough.

GINGER HAIR?

Other things, such as how tall we are, depend on lots of genes we inherit from our parents but also other factors, such as what we eat.

Things such as playing musical instruments, being good at drawing or learning different languages is even more complicated. Genes may be important here but other things such as practising at a young age and enjoying it also play a big role.

The more we like things the more we practise and the better we get. It's not always about your genes.

HOW MUCH DO OUR GENES AFFECT US?

Why is my best friend so tall!?

Why do some people grow really tall whereas others are much shorter? We know that we tend to have a similar height to our parents and this is partly due to the genes they pass on. However, the **food** that we eat and how we **sleep** also affects our height.

I just want to play something other than basketball, that's all.

Food gives us the **energy** to grow and when we are asleep, our brain releases a chemical messenger called **growth hormone**, which helps our cells grow and divide.

We also know from records that people a hundred years ago were on average several centimetres shorter than us. That is not enough time for evolution to make a big difference, so we know that genes are not the only thing controlling height.

You are a mixture of your genes and your environment

Experts think that everything about us, including how tall we are, the way we look, how we think and even our health, is due to a combination of genes and our surroundings, or our **environment**. We inherit about 20,000 genes from our parents but other factors, such as our food, the exercise we take, what **diseases** we catch, and the **weather** where we grew up, will also have an impact on how our bodies and minds develop.

SPOT A RELATIVE 500 YEARS!

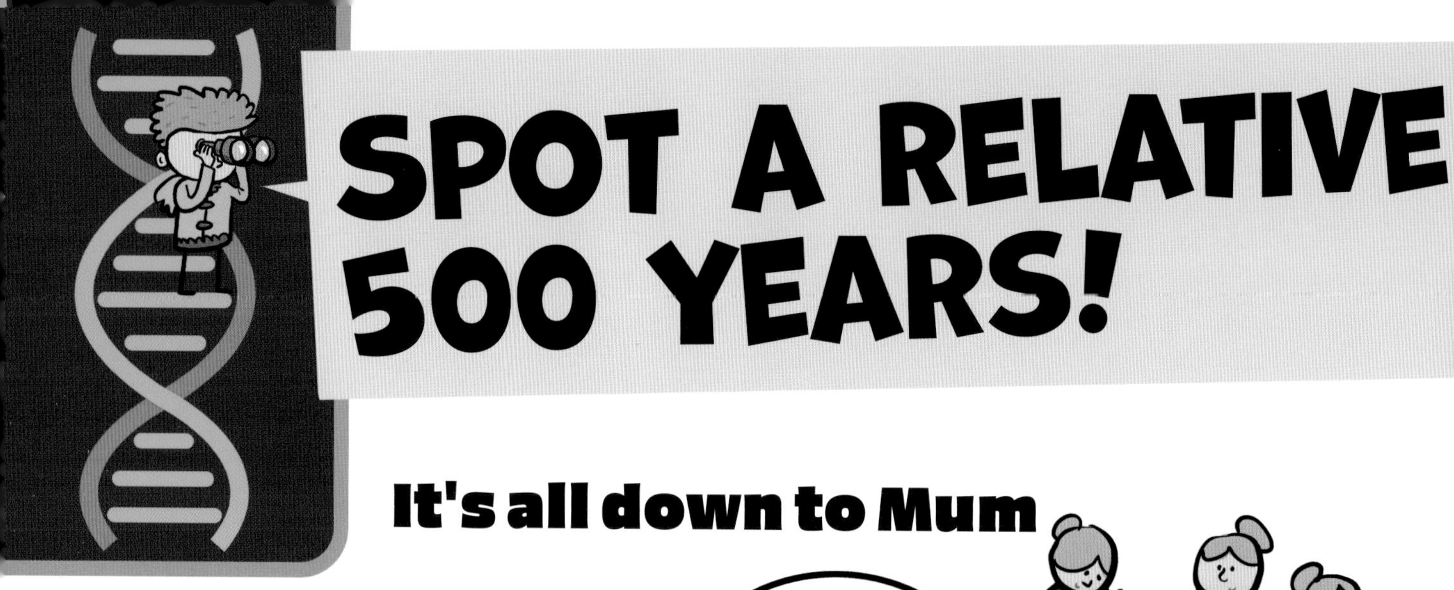

It's all down to Mum

Where are you great-granny?

We can work out if somebody is a close relative from their DNA. However, every time DNA is transferred from parents to a child, it gets mixed up. After each generation it gets harder to spot who is related. The genes from your eight great-grandparents are so jumbled up that their DNA code looks a lot like a stranger's. It is difficult to track family DNA back more than about 150 years.

However, our mothers help out by giving us a piece of DNA identification.

AFTER

We receive a small **extra piece of DNA** from our mothers. This is not stored in the nucleus but in parts of the cell called **mitochondria**. These are the energy factories in our cells.

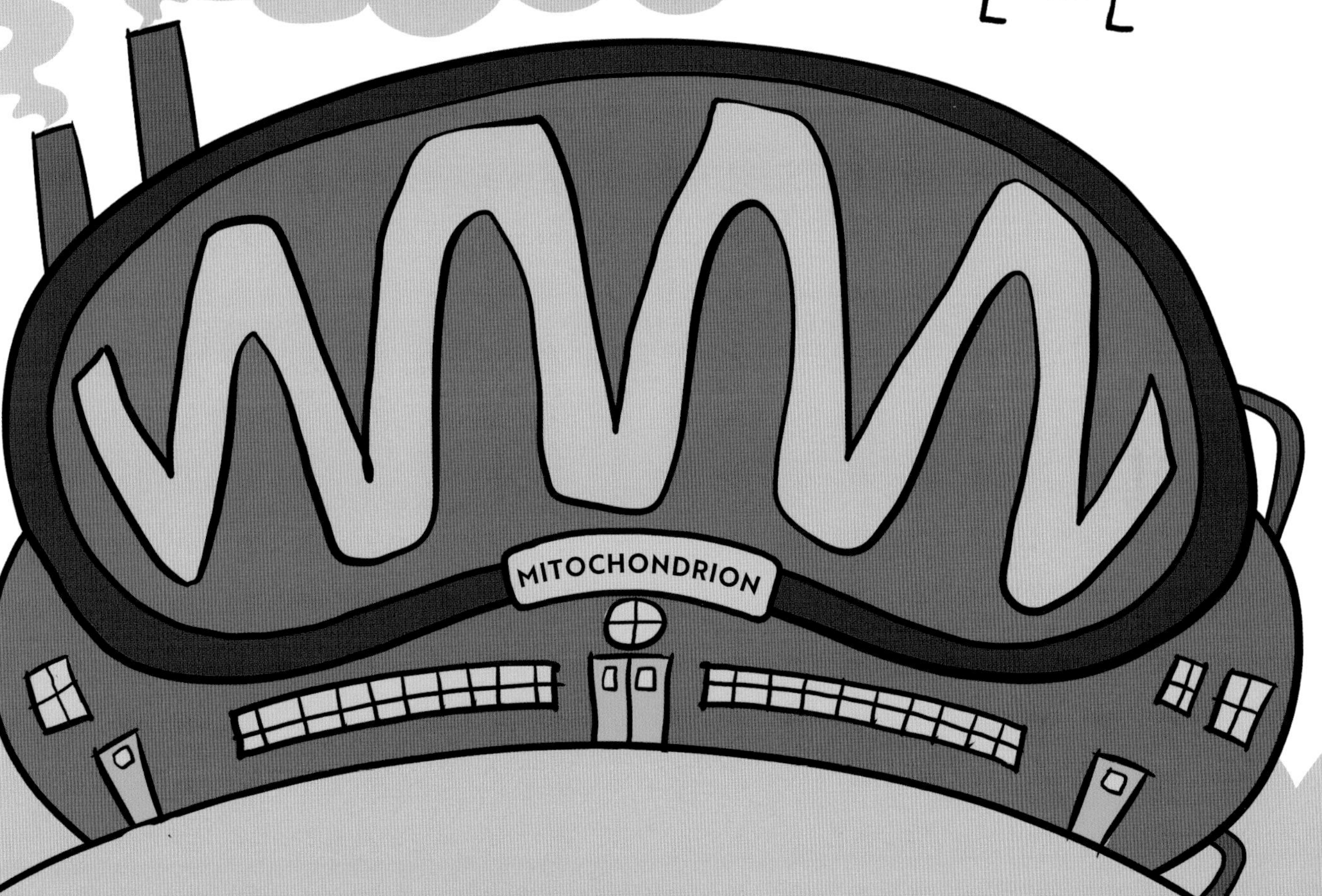

Family tree tracker

Your mum inherited her mitochondria from her mother and your grandmother got her's from your great grandmother. As this DNA rarely changes, it means you can track DNA through the mother's line for hundreds of years. This is a really good way of tracking family trees and seeing who is related to each other.

TRAFFIC LIGHTS GREEN! BLUE?

Why is there blue in traffic lights?

There are some interesting genes on the X chromosome. Females always have two copies of these genes because they have two X chromosomes. Men pass on their Y chromosome to their sons, so males only have one copy of these **'X-linked'** genes. This means if a man has a **mutation** on an X-linked gene, he does not have a spare working copy and that can cause problems.

Men's problems

Because of this genetic difference between males and females, there are several **genetic problems** that are more common among men than women. Women don't have these problems (or only very rarely). Even though they may have the faulty gene, they normally have a spare copy that is correct.

RED!

Lost colours

A common X-linked problem is **red-green colour blindness**. About 1 in 20 men have this feature, which means their eyes cannot tell the difference between the colours red and green.

This could cause problems at **traffic lights**! It is now common for the green Go signal to have blue light mixed in so people with colour blindness can still tell it apart from the red Stop signal.

Free kick to the reds ... er ... greens ... reds ... I mean to this team!

Mum
XX
Dad
XY
Son
XY
I am colour blind.

Colour blindness is **carried by mothers**, who are unaffected. If you are colour blind it might be interesting to ask about your **mum's brother** or **aunt's sons** to see if any of them are colour blind as well.

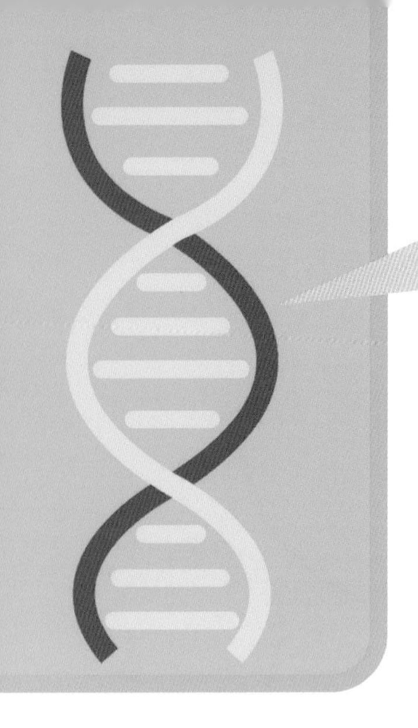

GENE ON, GENE OFF

Which genes are being used?

Even though the DNA is the same in every cell, the body is made up of many very **different kinds of cell**. For example, a blood cell looks nothing like a brain cell or a muscle cell. This is all due to the way genes are switched on and off in different cells. Each type of cell just uses the genes that make the proteins for their particular job.

We have the same genes!

Recruit Number 13, 214 ... Muscle
BONE

Our DNA makes proteins that control which genes are being switched on and which ones are shut down. Some of these proteins fold our DNA into tight knots which mean the DNA can't be opened up and read.

There. Now try and undo that knot!

Tying up DNA like this creates changes in the way different genes work. However, the DNA code has not been changed. This system is called **epigenetics**, and scientists are just beginning to learn how it works.

Get set! Go!

One way epigenetics works is to attach proteins to particular places on the DNA, called **trigger point promoters**. These are like sports coaches training Olympic athletes. The coach gets the athletes ready to start a race, and the trigger point promoters in our DNA tell a particular gene to get ready to switch on to make a human – and off again when it is no longer needed.

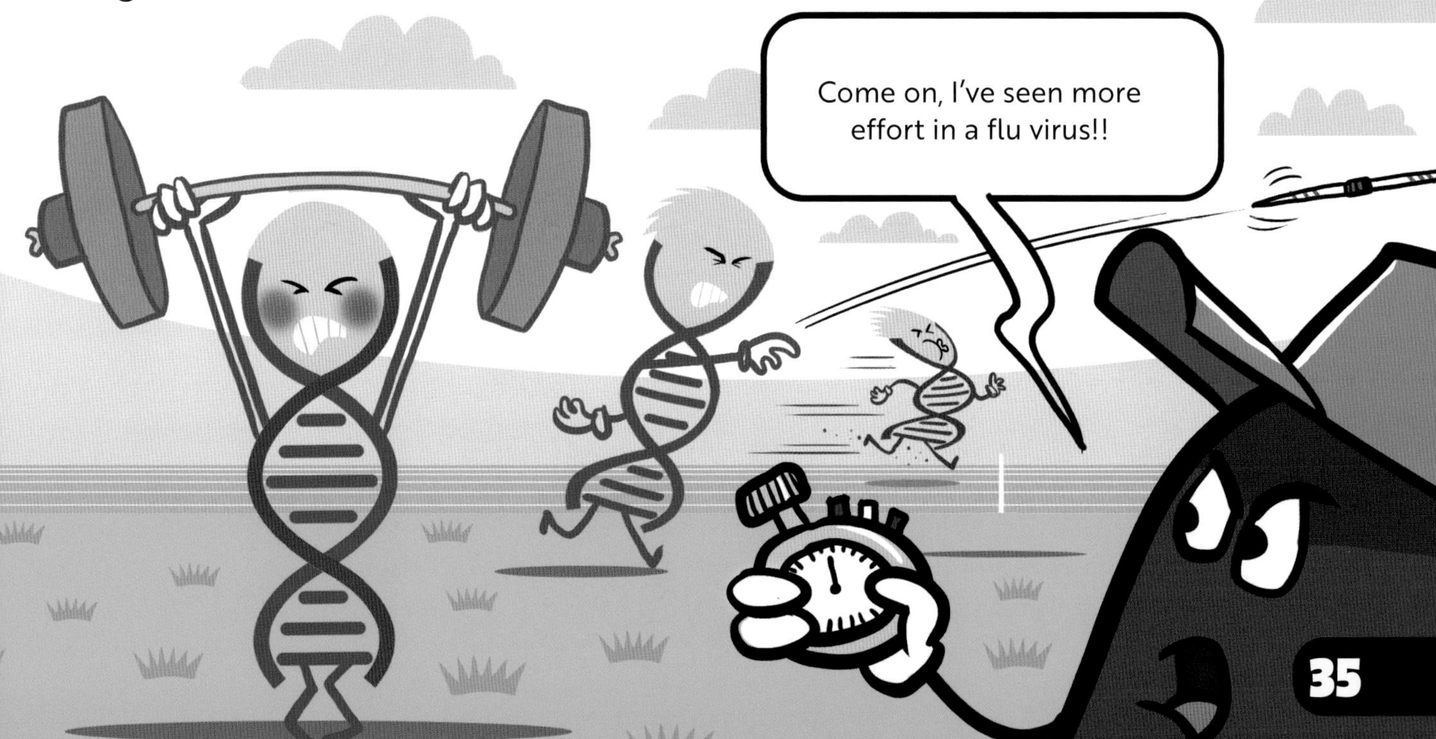

Come on, I've seen more effort in a flu virus!!

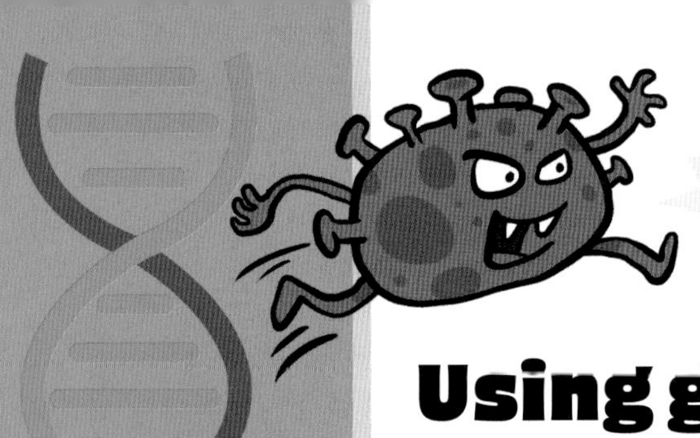

DNA THAT

Using genetics to understand, track and treat viruses

You can't just sit around all day. You should be out there infecting people like your sister.

Viruses are one of the laziest things on Earth. **It is hard to know at times if they are even alive or dead.**

They contain DNA (or **RNA**, a very similar chemical) but they can't move or even copy themselves to make new viruses. Some of them, like the virus that causes **covid-19**, can't even be bothered to form a double helix like all other kinds of life form. They have just a single strand of code.

That looks like SO much work.

Cell invader

Viruses have a **sticky chemical coat** that waits for passing cells to brush past it so it can have a free ride. Once attached to a cell, the virus injects the DNA strand into the cell, where it then forces the cell to make copies. **Eventually the cell is so full it bursts, releasing more viruses to attack other cells.**

MAKES DISEASES

Viruses try to hide inside cells to stay away from **defenders** in our blood called **white blood cells**. The white blood cells eventually make chemicals called **antibodies** which help to destroy viruses.

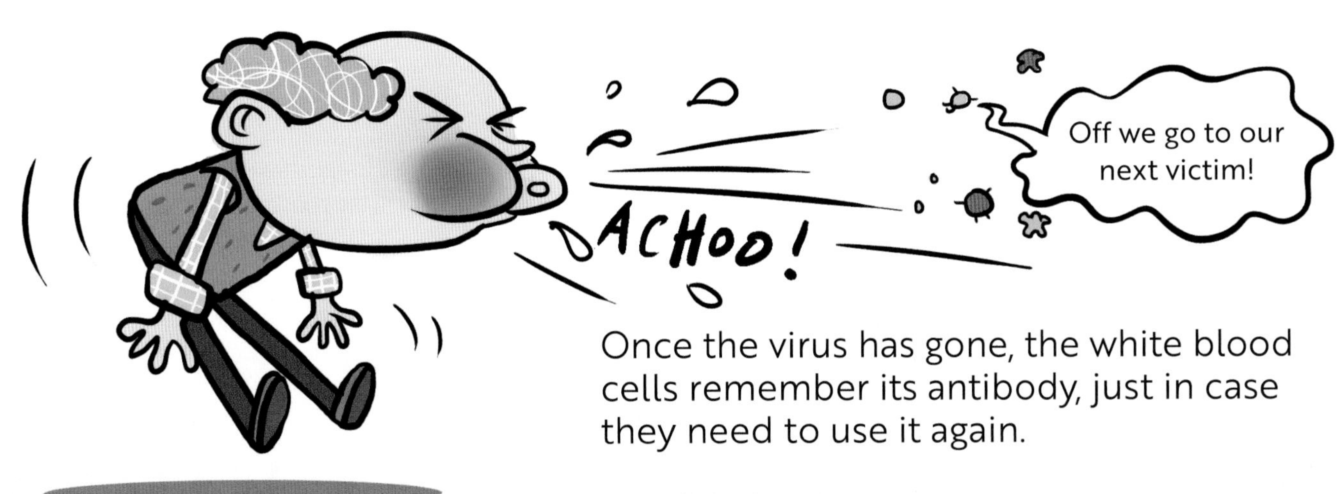

ACHOO!
Off we go to our next victim!

Once the virus has gone, the white blood cells remember its antibody, just in case they need to use it again.

Can a vaccine help?

White blood cells can be taught to spot viruses they haven't seen before using **vaccines**. Vaccines are similar to the viruses but they don't make us sick. Vaccines help produce antibodies that then wipe out the invaders.

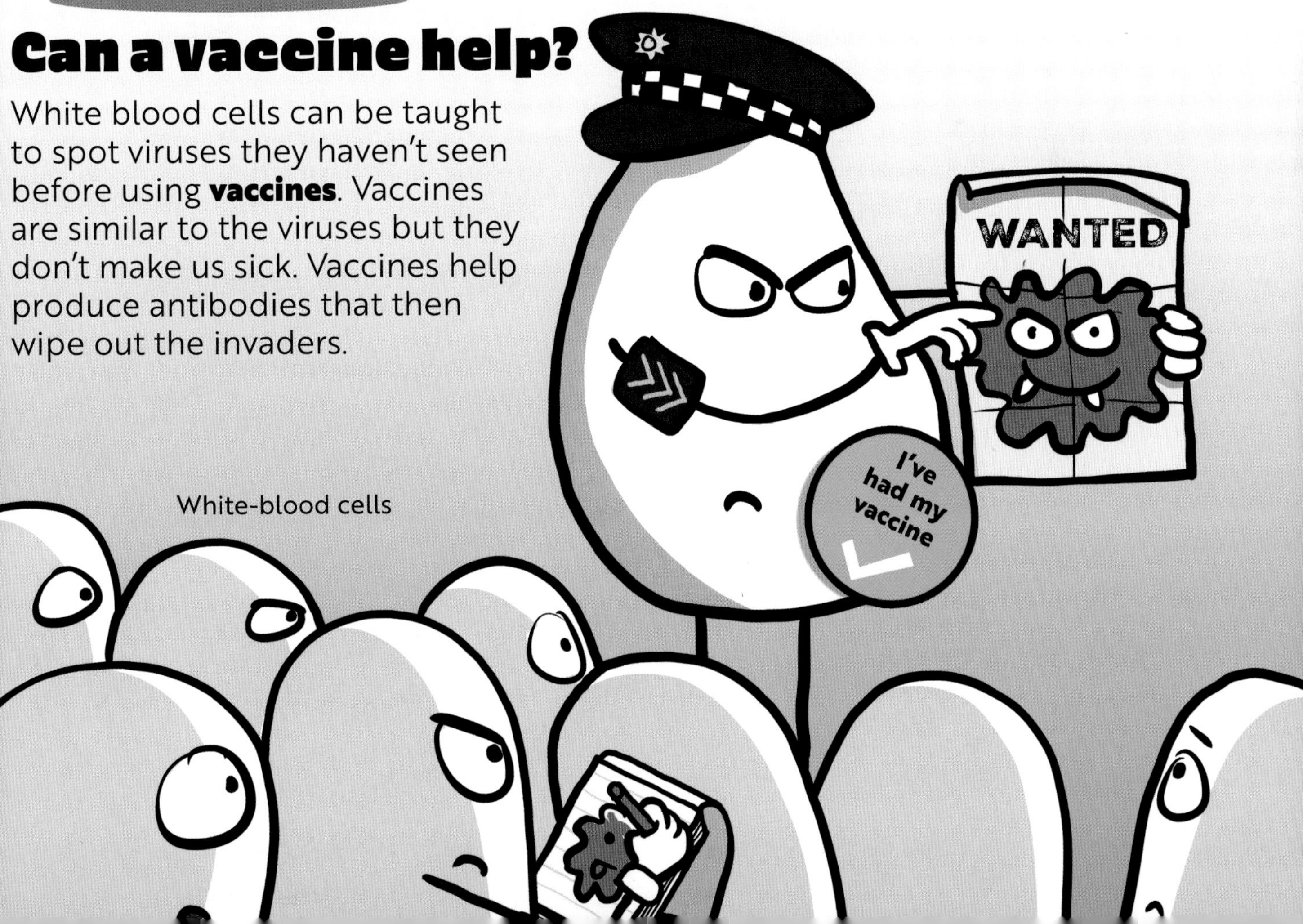

White-blood cells

WHO DID IT!?

Using DNA to solve crimes!

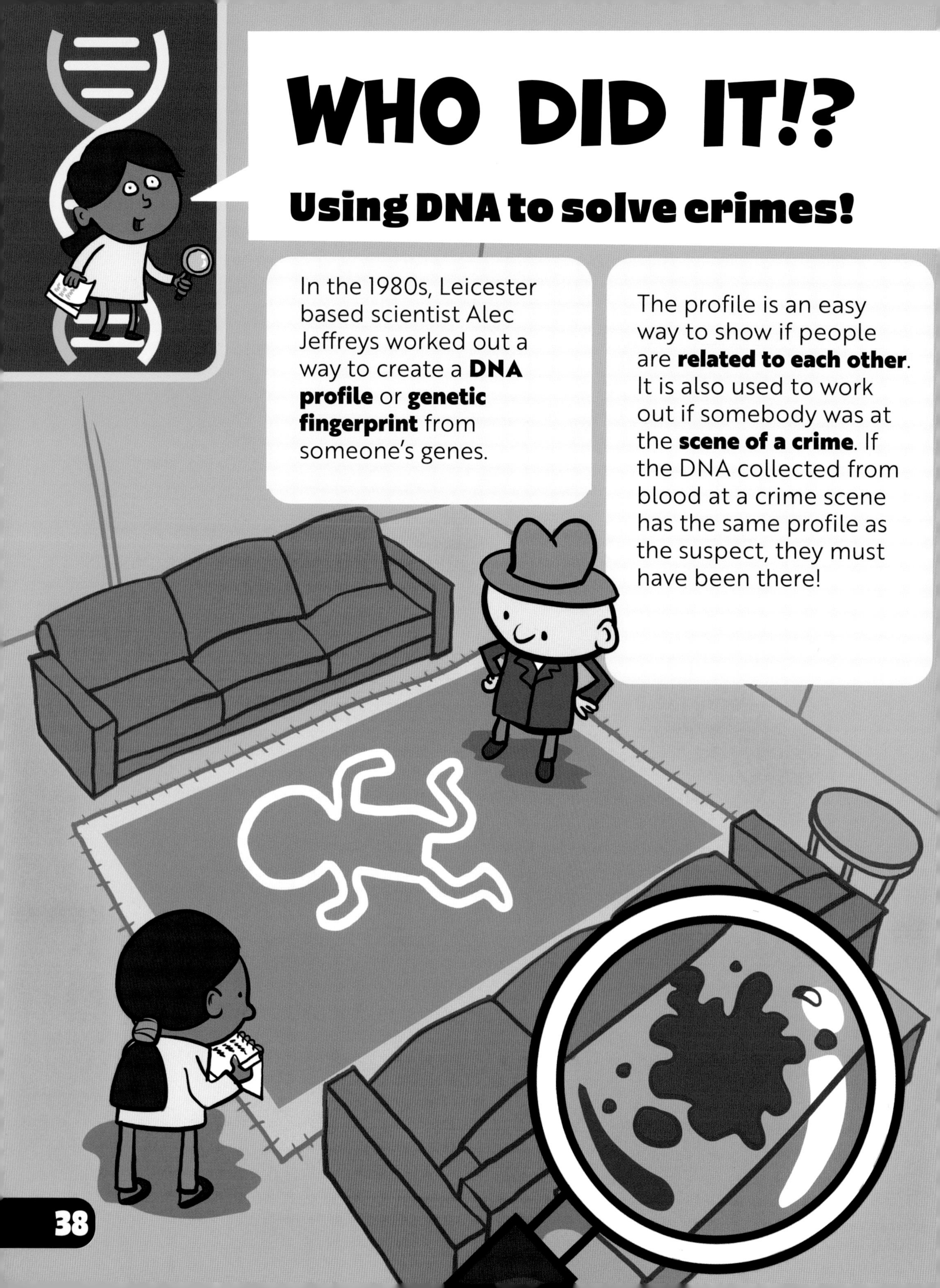

In the 1980s, Leicester based scientist Alec Jeffreys worked out a way to create a **DNA profile** or **genetic fingerprint** from someone's genes.

The profile is an easy way to show if people are **related to each other**. It is also used to work out if somebody was at the **scene of a crime**. If the DNA collected from blood at a crime scene has the same profile as the suspect, they must have been there!

The full profile can be created today by looking at the sequence of letters in DNA. However, back in the 1980s it was not possible to read DNA like this. Alec noticed that we all had a different number of **repeated sequences** in our DNA. These can be cut up and separated in a laboratory to create unique chunks. The chunks can then be shown as stripes of different thicknesses on coloured gel. Experts compare the patterns of stripes to figure out who's DNA it is. Maybe it matches the DNA left behind by a criminal.

DNA profiles have been used to help convict thousands of people – and to let innocent people go free!

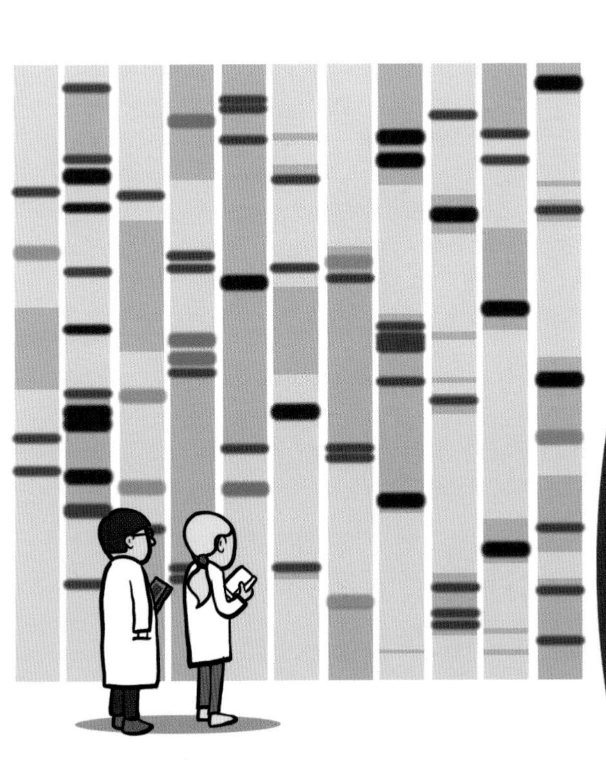

WHO IS IN CHARGE?

DNA improves our lives

Our DNA has **evolved over millions of years** to cope with the problems and threats that would otherwise make it hard to survive. To stay alive, have babies and raise our own children we need to find food, shelter, warmth and be able to protect ourselves. If our DNA does not help us to do this, we'll die and our DNA is not passed onto the next generation.

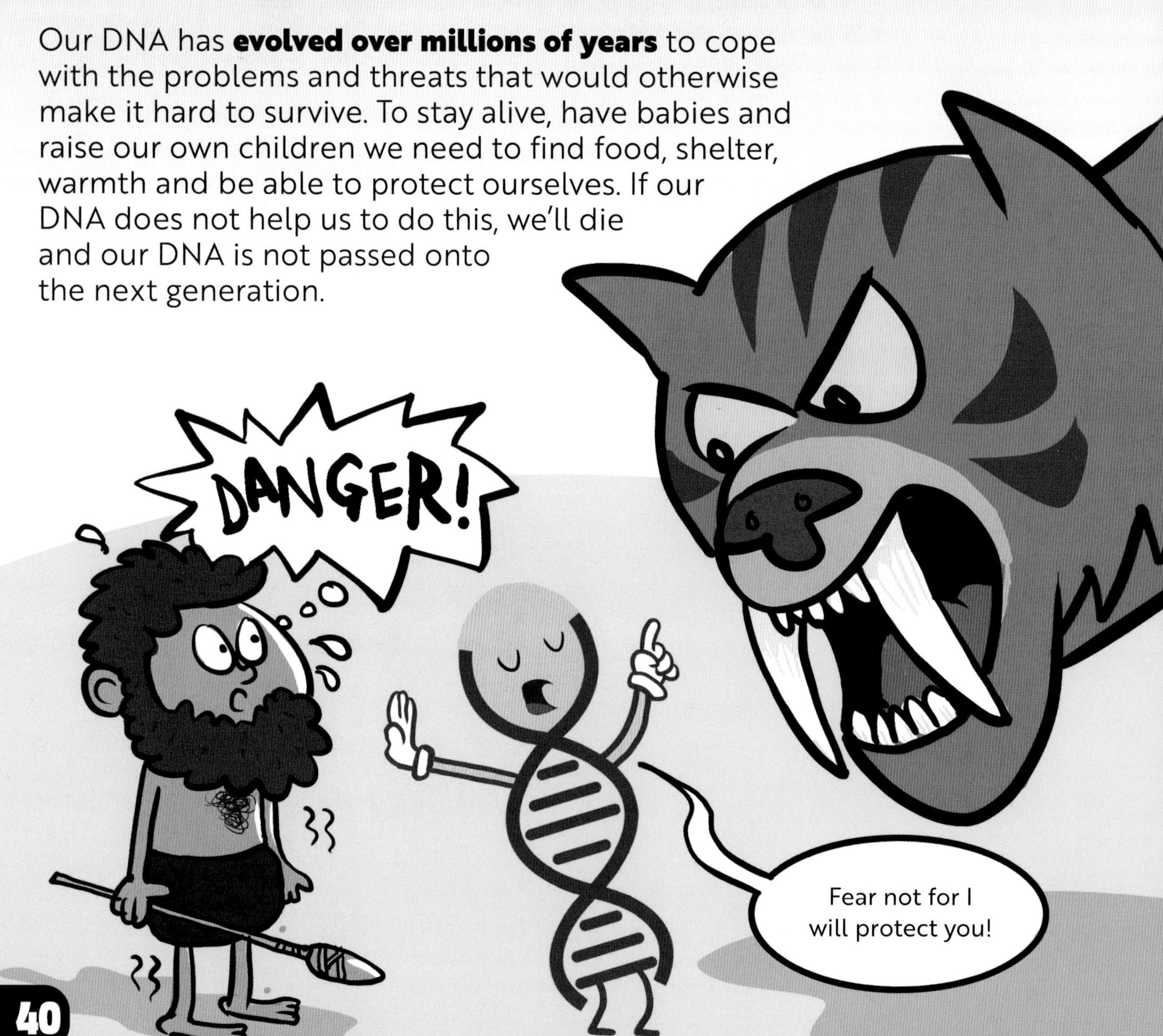
DANGER!
Fear not for I will protect you!

Old genes, new lifestyle

Successful genes that got passed on are the ones that made us look out for danger and eat lots of food when it was available (because often there was no food at all). Today, the way we live is changing faster than evolution can keep up with. Over the last few centuries we have got much better at creating safe places to live with a good supply of food.

Have you seen what they're saying about us on social media?!
Homework
TikTok
Snapchat
Texts
Gossip

Our DNA has prepared us to hunt and gather food and find a safe shelter. It hasn't had time to adapt to supermarkets and social media yet! Our DNA doesn't control us but knowing what it does will help us understand how we think and feel.

YOUR DNA: OUR STORY

WHAT IS DNA?

You have read that DNA is a chemical held inside cells that contains the instructions for making a new living body. All life uses DNA, and it is passed from parents to offspring. Over millions of years, the instructions, or genes, change slowly so living things are better able to survive as their environment changes. This slow process is called evolution, and it has made all living things from us humans to all animals, plants and mushrooms.

DNA contains the hidden language of life, that can be read in blocks of three letters by special code breakers to organise amino acids into proteins. You now know that DNA splits in half so it can be copied, and that cells can divide.

You have grasped that all living things are connected to the great tree of life, and that our DNA is passed onto our children alongside that of our partner. That makes new life from a brand new mixture of genes that is always different from our own. This gives our children a better chance to cope with the changes in the world around them.

You now understand that our DNA may help explain why we look the way we do or have some of our natural talents, but it doesn't tell us what to do or how we live our lives.

What can you do when you have cracked the code?

There are many types of jobs that you can get if you understand the language of life and the story of our DNA. These include solving crimes, detecting and treating viruses and diseases, improving food production and explaining how we are all related to each other and other living things.

TAKE THE DNA QUIZ!

Do you have what it takes to be a professor of clinical genetics?

1. How many letters are needed to make the code for one amino acid? **A** 1, **B** 2, **C** 3 **D** 4

2. How many different letters are there in DNA? **A** 1, **B** 2, **C** 3 **D** 4

3. What type of structure does DNA make?
A circle, **B** square, **C** double helix

4. Where in the cell is the DNA stored?
A nucleus, **B** mitochondria,
C endoplasmic reticulum

5. Which of these is autosomal dominant? **A** height, **B** hating bitter vegetables, **C** colour blindness, **D** rolling your tongue

6. Which of these is autosomal recessive? **A** height, **B** hating bitter vegetables, **C** colour blindness, **D** rolling your tongue

7. A gene is ... **A** a protein, **B** a strand of DNA, **C** the code for making a protein

8. The letter A forms a link with ... **A** T, **B** C, **C** G?

9. Who discovered natural selection? **A** Alec Jeffreys, **B** Charles Darwin, **C** James Watson **D** Francis Crick

10. Who always gives you your mitochondrial DNA?
A Dad, **B** Mum, **C** Grandad

11. How many chromosomes do we have in each of our cells?
A 20, **B** 23, **C** 46

12. Who do men inherit their Y chromosome from? **A** their mum, **B** their dad, **C** their mum's father, **D** their father's father

The answers are on page 48.

GLOSSARY:

What does it all mean!

Amino acids: small chemicals that are brought together by the RNA code breakers to build proteins. They tend to be made of carbon, nitrogen, hydrogen and oxygen. Some of these we can make ourselves but others we get from our diet.

Ancestor: someone or something older that is related to you through your parents and might have died.

Antibody: a type of protein produced by the body to recognise, attach to and help kill harmful substances like viruses.

Autosomal dominant: a type of inheritance whereby either parent has a gene change and can pass it on to either their son or daughter.

Autosomal recessive: a type of inheritance where both parents have to have a change in the same gene and then both pass this on to either their son or daughter.

Cell: the smallest part of the body that is able to divide. Our first cell is formed when the egg and sperm join at conception.

Chemical: a particular substance.

Chromosome: how our genes are packed together in the nucleus.

Clinical genetics: the study of inherited diseases and problems.

Covid-19: a disease caused by a virus that appeared in 2019.

Dad: a parent that passes on a X chromosome to his daughter and Y chromosome to his son.

Dinosaur: a type of reptile, often large and fierce, that lived between about 250 and 66 million years ago.

DNA: a long strand of 4 letters or bases (A, C, T or G) attached to each other by a special sugar inside the nucleus. It binds to a second strand that acts as a mirror to keep it strong and twists into a tight double helix. DNA is short for the full name: deoxyribonucleic acid.

Double helix: how two strands of DNA are linked to each other.

Embryo: when the egg and sperm join together to create the beginning of a baby. At about ten weeks until birth this is called a fetus.

Endoplasmic reticulum: A network of tubes inside a cell where proteins and other useful chemicals are made.

Energy: the ability to move or do something.

Environment: where living things breathe, move, eat and reproduce.

Epigenetics: the science that studies how genes are switched on and switched off in different conditions.

Evolution: how random DNA changes alter whether an organism is likely to survive and reproduce successfully.

Extinct: when a particular type of living thing is no longer able to find a mate and have offspring (children) and so dies out.

Gene: part of the DNA that has the code to make a particular protein.

Generation: the organism produced from its parents until it grows up and has its own offspring with a new partner. Grandparents, parents and children are three generations.

Genetic fingerprint: a unique pattern made by cutting up DNA into smaller chunks based on the size of particular repeat sequences found throughout our DNA which are different in everybody apart from identical twins. It is a bit like breaking a large book down into chapters of different sizes.

Genetics: the study of genes and the way they are inherited.

Hormone: a chemical message released into the body to adjust the internal conditions of the body often so they are better suited to the environment around us at that particular time.

Inheritance: how features or conditions are passed on in families.

Mammal: an animal that feeds its young on milk. Most have hairy bodies.

Meiosis: when a cell copies its DNA and divides in four in the sexual organs so that either sperm can be made in males and eggs in females. These then meet to form the beginnings of a new life.

Mitochondria: the powerhouse centre of the cell that provides energy. They also contain some DNA and we inherit them from our mother.

Mitosis: when a cell copies its DNA and splits in two to make two perfect copies of itself. This takes place throughout the body as we grow.

Molecule: chemicals joining together in a tight partnership.

Mum: a parent that passes on the X chromosome to her offspring.

Mutation: a change in the DNA code meaning that the protein it codes for can no longer be made in the same way.

Natural selection: a theory of evolution whereby only the organism most adapted to the environment will survive and find a mate to have offspring and pass on its DNA.

Nucleus: the part of the cell that stores our DNA.

Organism: an independent life form such as a human, plant, fungus or bacterium.

Parent or care-giver: A person that may have passed on their DNA to their child and tends to look after them.

Protein: a chemical coded by genes that works like a machine to build and repair the body.

Ribosomes: These are the code breakers that help read the DNA code and translate this into proteins.

Sequence: the letters of the DNA code when read out.

Sperm: a type of swimming seed produced by the biological father that joins with an egg from the biological mother to create an embryo.

Trigger point promoters: chemicals that prepare genes to be switched on.

Vaccine: a chemical or a virus that has been made harmless, which is given to a person to train the body to recognise and kill other potentialy dangerous viruses.

Virus: something that can be passed on from one living thing to another (infectious) and includes either DNA or a shorter similar molecular RNA wrapped in a coat, made of protein. It can often make you feel unwell.

White cell: part of the blood's defence team to spot and kill viruses.

INDEX

Quiz Answers

1. C 3 **2.** D 4 **3.** C double helix **4.** A Nucleus *and* B mitochondria **5.** D rolling your tongue **6.** B hating bitter vegetables **7.** C the code for making a protein **8.** A T **9.** B Charles Darwin **10.** B Mum **11.** C 46 **12.** B Their dad

What was your score?

0-3 Perhaps you want to read the book again. **4-6** Good stuff, you are on your way.
7-9 Wow, you are almost ready for university. **10-12** Incredible, it won't be long before you are writing your own book!

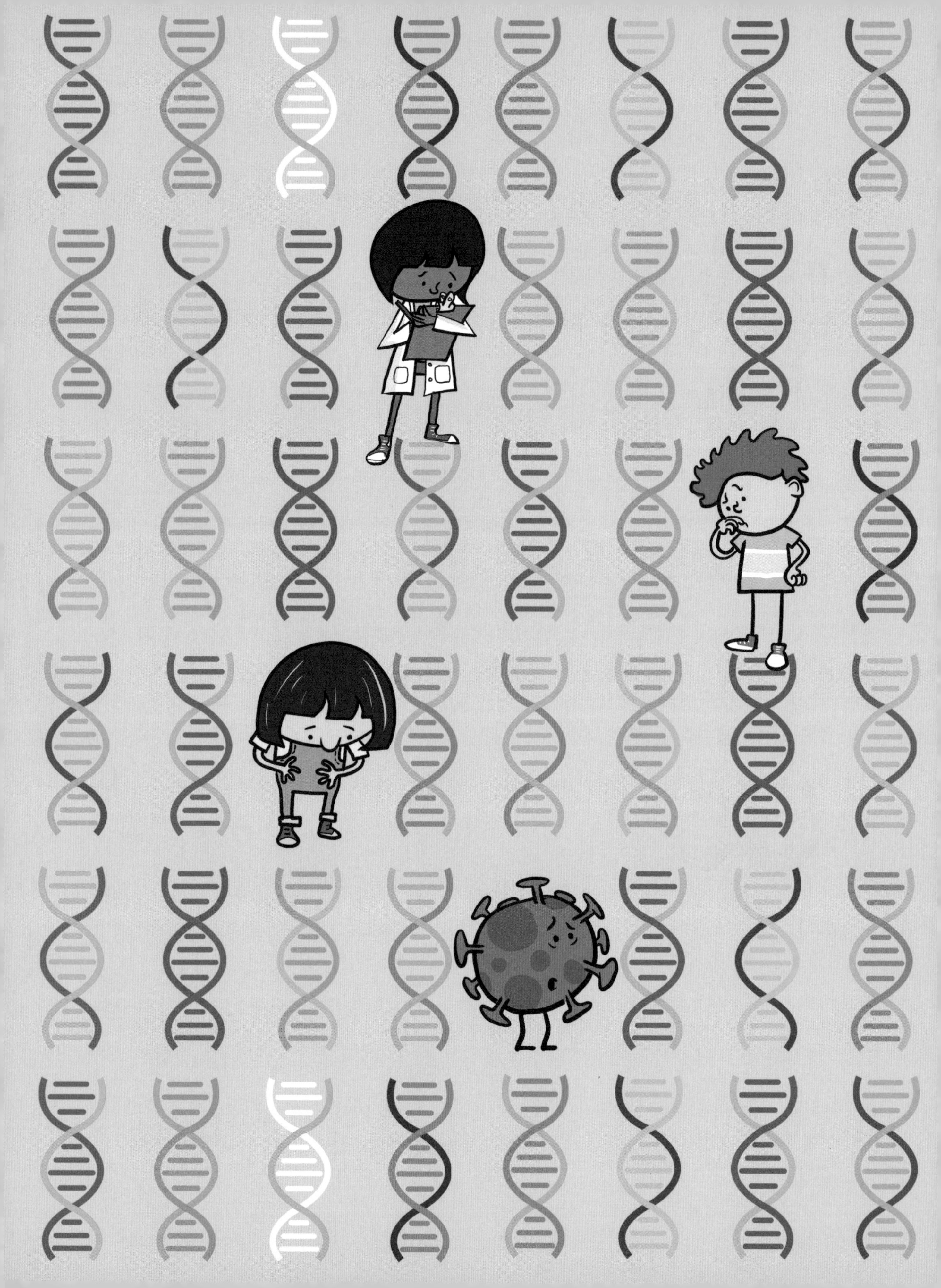